Press for Success

Secrets for Precise and Speedy Quiltmaking

Myrna Giesbrecht

That Patchwork Place

Press for Success

© 1996 by Myrna Giesbrecht

That Patchwork Place, Inc., PO Box 118, Bothell, WA 98041-0118 USA

Printed in the United States of America
01 00 99 98 97 96   6 5 4 3 2 1

CREDITS

Technical Editor	Melissa Lowe
Managing Editor	Greg Sharp
Copy Editor	Tina Cook
Proofreader	Melissa Riesland
Design Director	Judy Petry
Text and Cover Designer	Sandy Wing
Production Assistant	Shean Bemis
Illustrator	Laurel Strand
Illustration Assistant	Lisa McKenney
Photographer	Brent Kane
Photography Assistant	Richard Lipshay

ACKNOWLEDGMENTS

None of the quilts in this book would have been completed on time if it weren't for the delightful and extremely talented Carol Seeley, who quilted all the quilts in just twenty-one days. She's a wonder! They're lovely; thanks a lot, Carol.

DEDICATION

Five years ago, when I gave up trying to compete in the corporate rat race and headed home to start my own business, I decided I needed role models. It's been my experience that the best way to achieve a goal is to find a role model who lives as you want to; then work out a game plan following your model's example. The quilting industry is full of wonderful, talented individuals—most of whom are willing to help you along. I chose the following women because they each challenged me to improve and excel in their particular areas of expertise. Therefore, I could not have written this book without them.

Many thanks to:

Nancy J. Martin, whose presentation "Pieces of the Past" in Edmonds, Washington, some nine years ago inspired my love affair with the history of quilting and an appreciation for quilts as an art form. Nancy started me on my current path.

Mary Ellen Hopkins, whose zany sense of humor and wonderfully off-the-wall approach to quilting takes away the pressure of producing a masterpiece and just lets you enjoy, enjoy, enjoy.

Harriet Hargrave, whose excellence in the art of quilting has inspired and challenged me for years.

And to myself, a pat on the back for setting the goal, sticking with the game plan, and making it happen!

Library of Congress Cataloging-in-Publication Data
Giesbrecht, Myrna.
   Press for success : secrets for precise and speedy quiltmaking/ Myrna Giesbrecht.
     p. cm.
   ISBN 1-56477-136-9
   1. Patchwork. 2. Seams (Sewing) 3. Quilts. I.Title.
TT835.G53 1996
746.46—dc20
                      95-26023
                      CIP

CONTENTS

PREFACE

Before I took up quilting, my interests lay in the latest fashions and colors and in producing the most extensive wardrobe possible. In my mind, quilting was a long-forgotten, never-to-be-revived craft.

What I failed to comprehend was that quilting is an art. With my love of fabric, color, texture, and technique, it wasn't long before my passion for quilts and the art of quiltmaking took over my life. Now I don't have a thing to wear!

Unlike garment construction, macramé, knitting, counted cross-stitch, or any other craft I've tried, quilting continues to challenge my mind. There's always a new technique, a different design, or a fresh wave of colors and textures to explore; with each comes the chance to grow and develop personally and artistically.

As a quilter, I know that quilts soothe, exhilarate, mesmerize, and inspire the viewer. Quilters challenge, support, encourage, and teach one another. I encourage you to learn as much as you can and go as far as you want. What you create will touch not only you but those around you. I hope you have as much fun with the techniques in this book as I've had sharing them with you. Enjoy!

INTRODUCTION

Why write a book about pressing? This might sound corny, but it's because I became fascinated with "butting up"—making seam allowances lie snug against each other. In fact, I was so fascinated with this technique that I started butting shoulder and facing seam allowances on my blouses!

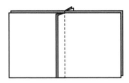

Seam allowances butt.

It all started when I first learned to quilt. I made a Trip Around the World quilt using the strip-pieced, Template-Free™ method. Following the directions, I was able to butt every seam allowance as I stitched the quilt top together. This made my first quilt a relatively hassle-free experience. In fact, because I tied it off, I completed the queen-size quilt in less than thirty hours. Quick, clean, and easy!

As I moved on to other projects, I discovered that not all instructions mentioned pressing and that some quilts were a nightmare to put together—with bulky seam allowances and mismatched design lines. Being a perfectionist, I soon became afflicted with what I call the "It's Gonna Butt No Matter What" (IGBNMW) syndrome, the sufferers of which try to butt each and every seam allowance in each and every quilt.

Pretty soon, I noticed common pressing patterns—what I call "traffic patterns"—and pressing solutions that could be used from one quilt to another. After that, I began to ignore quiltmaking instructions and the rules of pressing. I worked out pressing plans and constructed quilt tops based on my experiences and goals.

Then I found Donna Lynn Thomas's book *Shortcuts to the Top*. It's wonderful! Donna provides pressing details that make each of the designs much, much easier to put together. I wish all books were written like hers. But since they're not, I decided that quiltmakers needed a book devoted to the subject of pressing— one that would provide tips, tricks, and pressing patterns that could be applied to all quilt tops. And here it is!

TIP

Seams and Seam Allowances

The seam is the line of stitches that joins two fabrics. The seam allowance is the portion of fabric between the seam and the cut edge of the fabric. Most quilt patterns are based on a ¼"-wide seam allowance, which means the seam is ¼" from the cut edge.

GETTING STARTED

In *Press for Success* I've tried to show as many pressing scenarios as possible and to demonstrate the advantages of developing and using pressing plans. Pressing plans can make piecing your quilt tops quicker and easier, and neat, flat quilt tops are a lot simpler to quilt.

I can't overstress the importantance of reading the entire book. You'll find a guide to pressing, common pressing fallacies, and information on equipment and supplies. In "Pressing Plans" on pages 14–35, you'll find step-by-step instructions for developing pressing plans and examples of traffic patterns for several blocks, settings, and borders—progressing from simple to complex. These traffic patterns are used in many quilt designs. "Pressing Plan Exercises and Solutions" on pages 36–51 includes sample projects that you can use to practice before developing your own pressing plans.

By the time you finish reading this book, you'll have a clear understanding of how to press and how to develop and work through a pressing plan. It's pretty easy stuff. Once you've tasted the advantages of pressing plans, you'll be off and... pressing? I wouldn't be surprised if you start butting up your shoulder and facing seam allowances too!

PRESSING VS. IRONING

The words "pressing" and "ironing" may appear synonymous, but they're not. With ironing, you're out to conquer—grab that iron, throw it down on the fabric, wriggle it back and forth, and force those creases into submission. Pressing is more persuasive. With gentle, firm movements, you use the iron to direct the creases and correctly position the seams.

TIP

Pressing

When you're pressing, use smooth, gliding movements, and avoid wiggling or twisting the iron.

PRESSING FALLACIES

Tips and techniques are passed from quilter to quilter. Pretty soon they're treated as rules. Not rules with exceptions, but strong, steadfast, never-to-be-broken, cast-in-stone rules.

While there certainly should be guidelines to follow, we'd never progress as quilters if we didn't push the boundaries. Obviously these rules are meant to be broken!

Let's get rid of several pressing fallacies that can hinder rather than enhance our workmanship.

FALLACY #1

Press Toward the Darker Fabric

The first rule of pressing I learned was that all seam allowances are pressed toward the darker fabric. There are no exceptions.

Unfortunately, this philosophy has steered a lot of quilters away from using pressing plans. If you always press toward the darker fabric, you won't always be able to reduce bulky seams or butt your seam allowances.

Don't hesitate to press seam allowances toward the lighter fabric if it helps you reduce bulk and butt those seam allowances.

FALLACY #2

Never Press Seam Allowances Open

Have you ever been told that you must always press seam allowances to one side, never open? The reasoning is that the batting might beard and work it's way out through the seam.

Well, it might, but a poorly constructed batting might beard through the fabric too. To avoid bearding, use a quality batting.

No matter how diligent you are in putting together a pressing plan, there will be times when it's impossible to butt all the seam allowances. Rather than layer seam allowances, consider pressing one open. This will still provide a slight ridge for the opposing seam allowance to butt against.

Another solution is to flip one end of the seam allowance toward what would have been the correct direction. This produces a twist along the seam line which, in turn, causes an unsightly bump on the quilt top. When I use this technique I clip into the seam allowance at an angle and press each end flat, making the change in direction less obvious. I also apply a seam sealant, such as FrayCheck™, to prevent further fraying.

Press seam allowances open where multiple seams intersect, seam allowances layer, or seams are difficult to match.

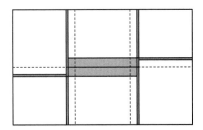

Press seam allowance open and butt.

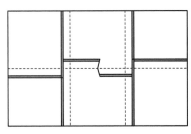

Clip and flip the seam allowance.

FALLACY #3
Never Use Steam

Have you been told that steam is bad stuff? Well, it's not. Overly aggressive pressing (or ironing)—not steam—causes blocks and strips to stretch out of shape. When used correctly, steam helps set the seam and keeps it crisp (assuming you are working with good-quality, 100% cotton fabric). Because it can be easier to distort fabric when using steam, beginning quilters may prefer to use a dry iron. Anyone confident of their pressing skills, however, should "turn on the steam."

FALLACY #4
Never Reposition Seam Allowances

Another fallacy is that once pressed, seam allowances should never be repositioned. It will be glaringly obvious should you try.

Well, it's better to get it right the first time, but don't leave a mistake just because "they" say it can't be changed. To re-press a seam allowance, refer to the directions on page 12 for setting and pressing a seam. Then press the seam allowance correctly, working gently and using steam.

FALLACY #5
Always Press from the Right Side

When you press from the right side, you can make sure that there are no creases or tucks along the seam line. Sometimes, however, it's easier to press from the wrong side than to try holding the seam allowance in place while flipping the quilt top around and over on the pressing surface—all the while attempting to maintain your sense of direction and make sure you're still in the right area.

Press from the wrong side when smoothing a wrinkled seam allowance or predesignating the direction of a seam allowance.

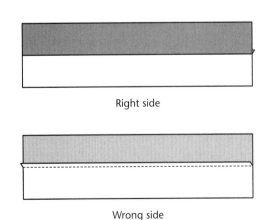

Right side

Wrong side

FALLACY #6
Pressing Replaces Accurate Stitching

Ever heard, "Oh, don't worry about it. You can fix it when you iron it"?

Nothing replaces accuracy. Either it's right or it's not. While it's possible to ease in a slight amount of fullness or smooth out minor puckering, it's impossible to eradicate glaring errors. If a seam is inaccurately stitched or a piece is too big or small, a much better approach is to correct the problem rather than trying to hide it with pressing.

TIP

Chain Piecing and Pressing

To assemble your quilt top faster, learn to chain piece and press. Determine how many of the same unit you need to sew, then stack these units in pairs. Stitch the pairs together in an assembly-line fashion, without stopping to cut the thread between the pairs. Press the pairs before you cut them apart.

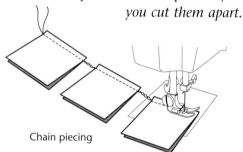

Chain piecing

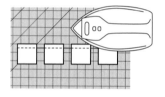

Align with guideline
on pressing surface
and set stitches.

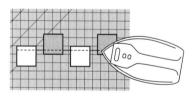

Turn every other pair
in the opposite direction.

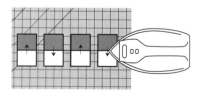

Fold over top fabric
and press in place.

PRESSING BASICS

Don't get caught up in a lot of do's and don'ts. Follow the procedure and use the tool or technique that helps you simplify construction, produce the most precise quilt top, and enhance your workmanship.

PRESSING EQUIPMENT

As vital as pressing is to quilting, there is little discussion of the equipment involved. It's a "bring-your-own-iron" type of thinking. But proper pressing equipment is as important as a sewing machine, rotary-cutting tools, and notions. Like all tools, pressing equipment should be chosen with personal taste, functional ability, and space limitations in mind.

IRON

Cost does not necessarily reflect a quality iron or the best iron for your needs. Since the repetitive function of pressing is one that can cause tendinitis or carpal tunnel syndrome, choose an iron that fits your hand and has a smooth, easily gripped handle, ergonomically designed to position the hand and arm. A light- to medium-weight iron will keep your arm from tiring too quickly.

The iron should also have easy-access controls, a large water reservoir, and plenty of steam vents. And personally, I'd never buy an iron with an automatic shut-off feature.

Clean the vents and soleplate of the iron regularly to remove any buildup of minerals, dirt, or starch products.

PRESSING SURFACE

Ironing boards were designed for ironing clothes. A large, flat pressing surface works much better for pressing the varied pieces of a quilt top. Either purchase a ready-made pressing board (see "Pressing Resource" on page 52) or construct your own, using a firm center material (such as wood), cotton batting, and muslin. To avoid constant repositioning, the surface should be wide enough to accommodate the 45" fabric width.

My favorite pressing surface is the Spaceboard™ from Voster Marketing, which has a cotton surface printed with a grid. When I'm pressing yardage, I position the entire width of the fabric over this surface. When I'm pressing strip sets, I position the raw edge of the seam allowance along one of the grid lines. Since cotton fabrics "stick" to each other, the strips stay in place while I press.

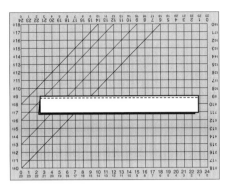

Spaceboard™

SPRAY BOTTLE

The spray bottle replaces the spray feature of the iron, which is often inadequate—it tends to "blop" rather than mist the fabric while using up the water reserves. Your spray bottle should have a fine setting for a light, even mist. Refill it with fresh water regularly. If you're recycling a bottle, make sure it is completely clean. Usually a squat, wide-based bottle is easiest to pick up and set down quickly.

SPRAY STARCH

Starch applied at the factory enhances the feel of fabrics and protects them from dirt and minor damage. This starch dissolves when you prewash, causing fabrics to lose their original crispness. To replace crispness or add extra body, apply spray starch when pressing prewashed fabrics. You also can apply spray starch to the completed quilt top during the final press to enhance its finished appearance.

PRESSING CLOTH

A pressing cloth may prevent shiny spots on dark fabrics, scorching, and water stains. A piece of 100% cotton muslin makes an excellent pressing cloth. For difficult wrinkles, dampen the pressing cloth to produce more steam.

When you press specialty fabrics, such as silk and lamé, always use a pressing cloth to prevent direct contact between the iron and the fabric.

SEAM SEALANT

Using a seam sealant, such as FrayCheck, on clipped seam allowances prevents fabrics from fraying further.

TIP

Caring for Your Iron

Using purified water in your iron will help keep it clean both inside and out, preventing dirt and chemical buildup. This may extend the life of the iron.

Pressing Height

More critical than the actual pressing surface is its height. Working with a pressing surface that is too high or low can lead to tendinitis, carpal tunnel syndrome, and back problems. Position the pressing surface so you can stand directly in front of it without leaning or twisting, and so you can move the iron comfortably in front of your body with your elbow slightly bent. This is virtually the same position you should use when typing, with the arms straight out from the body at the elbow, not reaching up or down.

If you'd prefer to press from a sitting position, adjust the height of the pressing surface to suit the position. Again, you don't want to be twisting, turning, or reaching up or down. I can't overstress the importance of matching the height of the pressing surface to your body proportions. Make the pressing surface work for you, not against you.

PRESS AS YOU GO

For best results, I recommend that you learn to "press as you go." This phrase, from garment construction, means that you press each seam allowance in place before moving on to the next step. This may be one seam allowance at a time or a series of seam allowances, as with chain piecing.

Constructing the blocks or the quilt top is simpler and more precise when seam allowances lie flat against the back of the fabric and the line of each seam is crisp and clean, without tucks or folds. The neater and more precise each seam, the easier the next one is to stitch and the more professional and attractive the finished product.

While it's always more accurate to press as you go, let's be realistic. Sometimes you've got more project left than time allotted. So, occasionally, you may want to use what I call the "Flip Flop" method. In a hurry, it's next best.

After you press the seam allowances in the first row, place the first and second rows right sides together. As you approach each intersection, flip the seam allowance in the second row in place. Use your fingertips to butt seam allowances. (See "Finger Pinning" on page 15.) Press the seam allowances before adding the next row.

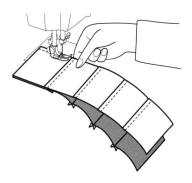

PRESSING YARDAGE

Flat, crisp yardage is important for every project. However, before pressing and cutting yardage, I recommend that you prewash to test for colorfastness, remove dirt and manufacturer's finishes, and preshrink the fabric. After you prewash the fabric, partially dry it in a dryer (or air dry). Press the fabric while it is still damp, before the creases set. The moisture provides the extra steam necessary to smooth out wrinkles.

1. Press the fabric on a smooth, even surface. (See "Pressing Surface" on pages 8–9.) Position the fabric so that it is piled in front, coming up and over the pressing surface and gently folding behind it. As you work, keep the fabric flat and smooth to prevent any additional wrinkling.

2. When pressing, gently smooth the iron over the fabric following the straight of grain. The movement is like gliding or skating. Do not use sharp arm movements. Simply glide the iron back and forth across the surface to smooth out any wrinkles. Avoid overworking the fabric.

    Pressing along the bias grain can stretch and crease the fabric. To remove a crease, mist the area lightly with water. Gently ease out the crease with your fingertips as you press.

    Avoid using the tip of the iron to work out creases; this specific and intense pressure further stretches the fabric.

Cutting and Pressing

Warning! Do not, under any circumstances, consider cutting pieces or strips from fabric that has not been pressed. The results will be totally inaccurate!

Prewashing and Storing Fabric

I prefer to work with prewashed fabrics, so I've made it a habit to wash fabric as soon as I bring it home. Since I'll need to press and store it anyway, I simply press it in half widthwise and then in half again before folding it lengthwise and storing. When I'm ready to begin a project, the fabric is washed, pressed, folded, and ready to cut.

Most of the time I cut a 5" charm square out of one corner to add to my collection, or a 5"-wide strip if I want to cut it up and send some to friends.

Tips for Strips

Mary Ellen Hopkins teaches a technique for pressing strips that works well.

1. Press one end of the seam allowance in place with the tip of the iron.
2. Place the strips right side up on the pressing surface. Position the tip of the iron along the seam allowance.
3. Lift the opposite end of the strips, using your fingertips underneath to hold the seam allowance. Hold the end slightly above the pressing surface, keeping the length of the strips fairly taut.
4. Move the iron along the seam in one continuous motion. The seam allowance will turn and press crisply and cleanly in place.

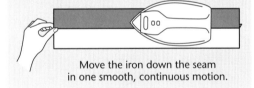

Move the iron down the seam in one smooth, continuous motion.

PRESSING SEAMS

When pressing seams, position the "excess" fabric of the seam allowance against the back of the block or quilt top with the same gentle gliding movement used to press flat yardage.

SETTING SEAMS

Before you press the seam allowance in place, you must set the seam. This makes it easier to turn over the seam allowance and helps smooth stitching puckers and eased fullness.

1. Lay the pieces or strips flat with the seam allowance toward the top of the pressing surface.
2. Gently place the iron against the seam line and seam allowance only and hold briefly in place. Avoid pressing the remaining fabric unnecessarily. Instead, lift and move the iron before pressing again.

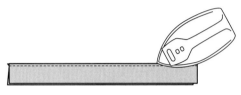

Press, lift, move, and lower the iron along the seam.

PRESSING SEAM ALLOWANCES TO ONE SIDE

1. Once you've set the seam, flip the top layer of fabric over. As you press, work your fingertips along the seam. Use your fingertips to ease the top layer of fabric over, to feel the bulk of the seam allowance, and to ensure that the top fabric and seam allowance remain flat against the pressing surface. Take care not to stretch the fabric.

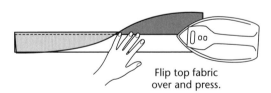

Flip top fabric over and press.

2. Gently press the top fabric over the seam allowance, moving the tip of the iron along the seam line. Use one continuous movement to press the seam allowance in place. Don't wiggle the iron back and forth.

PRESSING SEAM ALLOWANCES OPEN

Several of the same steps used for pressing seam allowances to one side are used for pressing them open.

1. Lay out the pieces or strips and set the seams as described in "Setting Seams" on page 12.
2. Open the piece or strip and place the fabric right side down on the pressing surface. Smooth the piece or strip on the pressing surface; it should lie flat.
3. Set the tip of the iron in the groove between the two fabrics and move the iron along the length of the seam, using one continuous motion. Work your fingertips in front of the iron to open the seam allowance and prevent creases from forming along the seam line.

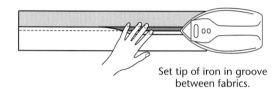

Set tip of iron in groove
between fabrics.

SPEED PIECING AND PRESSING

Rotary cutting and strip piecing help make quilting quicker, easier, and more accurate. Pressing plans based on these techniques further increase your speed and precision.

Wherever possible, incorporate speed-cutting and speed-piecing techniques. For example, look at the illustration below for making Connector Corner triangles. Methods like this one eliminate repetitive, time-consuming piecing while maintaining the flavor and design of the quilt top. Sounds good to me!

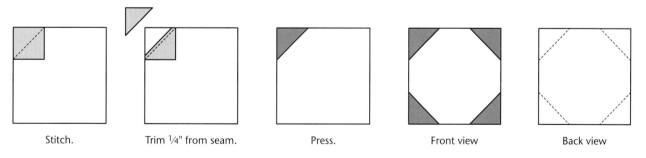

Stitch.   Trim ¼" from seam.   Press.   Front view   Back view

Connector Corner Method

PRESSING PLANS

A pressing plan closely resembles a construction plan, but a pressing plan focuses on the seam allowances.

Make:

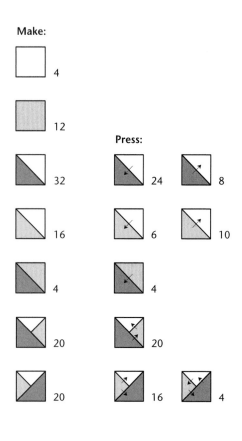

Press:

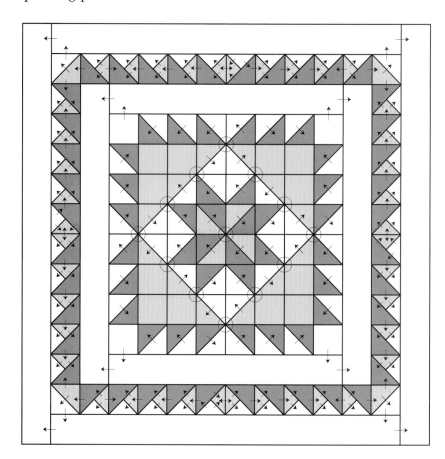

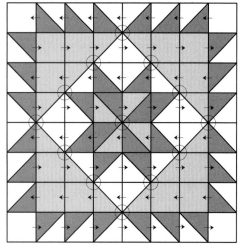

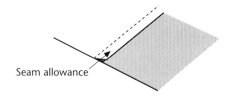

Seam allowance

The seam allowance is formed by two layers of fabric; these layers create bulk. One of the goals of a pressing plan is to evenly distribute the bulk created by the seam allowances. Bulky seam allowances can make it difficult to accurately piece the quilt top.

When the seam allowance is pressed to one side, there is a slight ridge along the seam line. This creates high and low sides of the seam. The bulk of the seam allowance is on the high side. If, when two seams intersect, the seam allowances have been pressed in opposing directions, the bulk of the seam allowances is distributed evenly. In addition, you can butt the two ridges against each other to hold the new seam firmly in place. Since butting seam allowances makes it easier and faster to stitch the quilt top, another goal of a pressing plan is to butt as many seam allowances as possible.

There's more to developing a pressing plan than directing the seam allowances to the left, right, up, or down. Fabric color, multiple intersections, angled seams, eight-point centers, and so on all need to be taken into account. In some instances it may be perfectly acceptable to press the seam allowance wherever it wants to go, but most times it's better to predetermine the direction by creating a pressing plan. When you make the pressing decisions in advance, you can use the seam allowances to help you create a flatter, more accurate, and easier-to-piece quilt top.

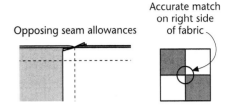

Opposing seam allowances

Accurate match on right side of fabric

Finger Pinning

Butting can take the place of pinning—allowing you to finger-pin each seam allowance as you stitch. It might take a while to sensitize your fingertips, but in the long run this technique saves time and improves accuracy.

To finger-pin:

1. Position two pieces with intersecting seam allowances, right sides together.
2. Slide the ridge of the top seam toward the bottom one until they are snug against each other (butting).
3. With your thumb and index finger, hold the pieces together on the new seam line and feel the joint. A heavy ridge indicates that the seam allowances are overlapped. A groove indicates that there is a space. The seams should be snug against each other.

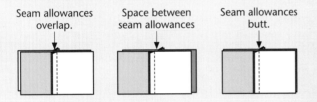

Seam allowances overlap.　　Space between seam allowances　　Seam allowances butt.

Hold the joint with your thumb and index finger until you have stitched the pieces together. If you are stitching a long seam with many intersecting seam allowances, handle each intersection individually. Position two pieces with intersecting seam allowances right sides together, seams butting. Stitch slightly into the seam and stop with the needle down. Finger-pin the first intersection as described above, then stitch through the intersection and stop with the needle down. Repeat this process for the remaining intersections.

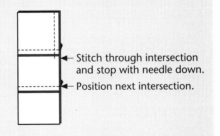

← Stitch through intersection and stop with needle down.
← Position next intersection.

If butting seams and finger pinning are new experiences for you, watch out for the "It's Gonna Butt No Matter What" syndrome. Before you know it you'll find yourself flipping seam allowances back and forth in your imagination—determined to make them all match perfectly. It just can't be done every time with every quilt. Occasionally you have to use another approach.

TIP

Using Your Presser Foot

As you sew, the presser foot pushes the top layer of fabric forward slightly. Try to position the top seam allowance so it faces the needle. The presser foot will push the top and bottom seam allowances together. You'll quickly find that this technique can't be used as often as you'd like, but use it whenever possible.

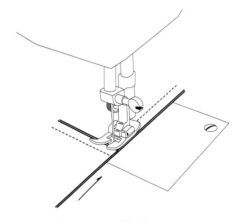

Whenever possible, face top seam allowance toward needle.

UNDERSTANDING PRESSING PLANS

The best way to develop a pressing plan is to work out from the smallest unit in the design. Once you've determined how the seam allowances should relate, you can develop a pressing plan that encompasses the entire design.

The first step in developing a pressing plan is to identify the smallest unit of each block within the design, then determine how its seam allowances relate to the surrounding seam allowances in the block. The second step is to determine how the seam allowances within each block relate to those in the surrounding blocks. The third step is to determine how the seam allowances within the rows relate to those in surrounding rows. The fourth step is to determine the direction of the seam allowances for the border(s).

Whenever you begin a project, think through each step in advance. Decide which direction you will press the seam allowances and why.

1. Redraw the blocks from the overall diagram on graph paper. As you work, use small arrows to indicate the pressing direction for each seam allowance.
2. Define the top, bottom, and sides for each block.
3. Determine the direction of any angled seams or rotating patterns in each block (see pages 20–22).
4. Determine the direction of the vertical seam allowances within each block.
5. Determine the direction of the horizontal seam allowances within each block.
6. Determine how many blocks you will make following each traffic pattern (see "Understanding Traffic Patterns" on page 19). There might be more than one traffic pattern for the same block.
7. Determine the direction of the vertical seam allowances between the rows of blocks.
8. Determine the direction of the horizontal seam allowances between the rows of blocks.
9. Determine the direction of the seam allowances within and between the borders.

Refer to the pressing plan as you stitch the quilt top together.

FOUR PATCH PRESSING PLAN

The following example illustrates the basic procedure for developing a pressing plan, beginning with the smallest unit, a Four Patch block, and working out to incorporate the entire quilt top.

1. Draw the Four Patch quilt on graph paper. As you work, use small arrows to indicate the pressing direction for each seam allowance.
2. Define the top, bottom, and sides for each block.

3. Determine the direction of the vertical seam allowances within each block. In this example, the best way to reduce bulk and butt the seam allowances is to press the vertical seam allowances toward the darker fabric. These seam allowances will butt against those in the blocks above and below when you join the rows.

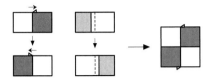

Press vertical seam allowances toward the darker fabric.

4. Determine the direction of the horizontal seam allowances within each block. If you press the horizontal seam allowance in every block in the same direction, you won't be able to butt the seam allowances when you join the rows. The solution is to press the horizontal seam allowances toward the top of the block for half the blocks and toward the bottom for the remaining blocks. When you assemble the rows, alternate the blocks. If the horizontal seam allowance in the first block is pressed toward the top, it should be pressed toward the bottom in the second block.

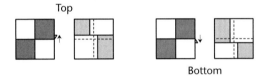

Press horizontal seams in opposing directions.

5. Determine the direction of the vertical seam allowances between the rows of blocks. Press the seam allowance between each block after assembling the rows. Press the seam allowances in odd-numbered rows to the left and in even-numbered rows to the right. When you join the rows, the vertical seam allowances will butt.

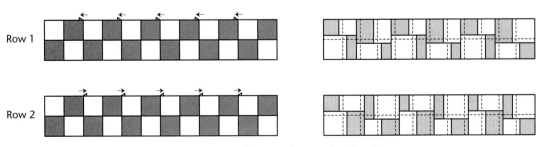

Press seam allowances in opposing directions.

6. Determine the direction of the horizontal seam allowances between the rows of blocks. Once you've joined the rows, press the seam allowances between the rows toward either the top or bottom of the quilt top. If you press the seam allowances that join the rows in opposite directions, the top will look bumpy and uneven. When you press the seam allowances in the same direction, the quilt top looks flat, even though each row is slightly higher on one side.

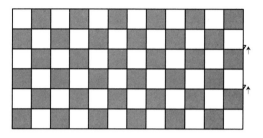
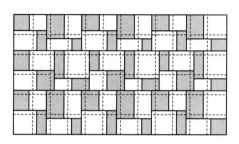

7. Indicate how many of a particular block is required and, of those, how many will be pressed in each traffic pattern. In this example, you need 48 Four Patch blocks and there are 2 different traffic patterns (24 blocks in each). Refer to the pressing plan as you assemble the blocks and quilt top.

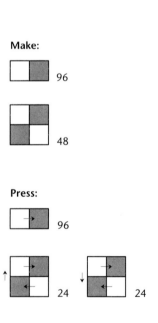

Make:

96

48

Press:

96

24   24

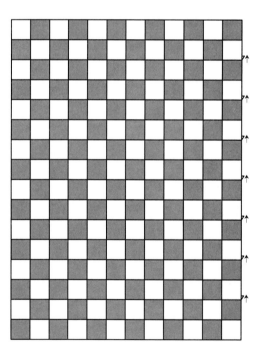

UNDERSTANDING TRAFFIC PATTERNS

The most practical approach to learning any new technique is to put theory into practice. This section includes traffic patterns for common quilt blocks, settings, and borders. Once you are familiar with these traffic patterns, you'll be able to develop pressing plans based on your specific project, goals, and experience.

BLOCKS

The majority of quilt designs are based on one or more blocks. These range from a simple Four Patch block to complex blocks containing diamonds, hexagons, and curves. Beginning with simple shapes and progressing to more complicated ones, this section illustrates basic pressing solutions and traffic patterns you can use when seam allowances intersect. Remember that the objective is to begin with the smallest unit in each block and work out to include the entire quilt top.

Squares and Rectangles

The easiest quilt patterns and pressing plans are based on squares and rectangles, which produce straight seams and 90° intersections.

Blocks such as Four Patch, Nine Patch, Tom's Patch, and Irish Chain are good examples.

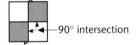
90° intersection

TIP

Emphasizing Your Design

When you press seam allowances toward a shape or area of your design, the ridges created by the seam allowances cause that shape or area to stand out on the quilt's surface. If you want to highlight a particular shape or area, press seam allowances toward it. If you want to keep a shape or area free for easier quilting, press seam allowances away from it.

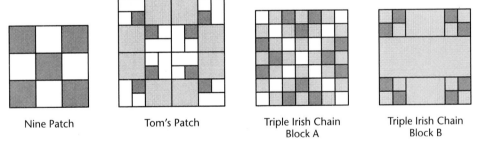

Nine Patch   Tom's Patch   Triple Irish Chain Block A   Triple Irish Chain Block B

These blocks are often speed-cut and -pieced using strip sets. Determine whether the seam allowances in all the strip sets need to be pressed in the same direction or whether some should be pressed in the opposite direction. Look at the following example for constructing a Four Patch block. The seam allowances on all the strip sets are pressed toward the darker fabric.

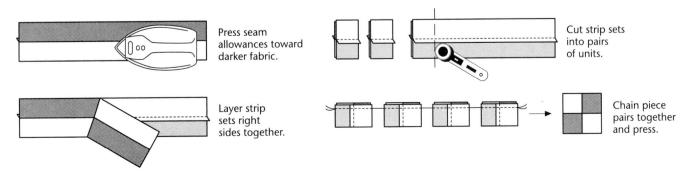

Press seam allowances toward darker fabric.

Cut strip sets into pairs of units.

Layer strip sets right sides together.

Chain piece pairs together and press.

TIP

Pressing Strip Sets

In her book Fun with Fat Quarters, *Nancy J. Martin has a wonderful tip for making and pressing small bias squares. This technique works great for any strip-pieced unit with closely spaced multiple seams.*

Simply place each seam on the edge of the pressing surface and press the seam allowances open or to one side, as needed. Let the seams you've already pressed hang over the edge of the surface while you press the next seam.

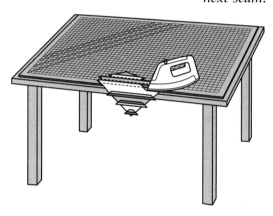

Triangles

Fortunately, not all quilts are made with simple squares and rectangles. Once you add triangles, developing a pressing plan becomes a bit more challenging. But it's worth it! When you butt seam allowances, matching, stitching, and producing sharp, narrow points is a breeze. You'll find yourself constructing more complicated blocks and quilts than ever—with greater ease.

While you're developing the pressing plan, remember to think about how you will stitch the pieces together. In blocks such as Hovering Hawks and Birds-in-the-Air, the diagonal seam allowances (the longest side of each triangle) don't intersect. If that's the case, you can press all of these seam allowances toward the darker fabric.

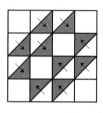 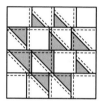

Hovering Hawks

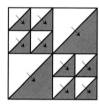 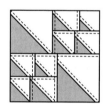

Birds-in-the-Air

In many blocks, the diagonal seam allowances intersect. The Flying Geese and Squares and Points blocks are good examples. If you press the diagonal seam allowances in each half-square triangle toward the darker fabric, you won't be able to butt the seam allowances when you stitch the units together. Instead, alternate the direction of the seam allowances as you press. Press the diagonal seam allowance on the first half-square triangle toward the darker fabric; then press the seam allowance on the second half-square triangle toward the lighter fabric.

Stack these half-square triangles according to the traffic pattern as you press. Be careful to note how many of each you need; sometimes you will need more of one than the other.

           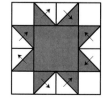 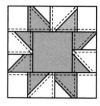

Flying Geese   Squares and Points

The more intricate a block, the more seam allowances you have to deal with. When you are planning a complex block, such as Shoo Fly, think about how the diagonal seam allowances above, below, and beside each other will intersect. Again, alternate the direction of the diagonal seam allowances as you press. Work through the block diagram in vertical and horizontal rows. Mark the direction of each seam allowance with small arrows. Each decision affects the next, as shown below.

Shoo Fly

Step 1	Step 2	Step 3	Step 4

Step 5	Step 6	Step 7	

Press:

8   8

Rotating Patterns

Many blocks are based on rotating patterns with intersecting seam allowances that converge at a central point or points in the block. (Don't confuse "central point" with the center of the block or quilt top; the central point might or might not be in the center of the block.) The LeMoyne Star, Diamond Star, and Shoo Fly blocks are good examples. In LeMoyne Star and Diamond Star, the seam allowances converge at one central point in the center of the block. In Shoo Fly, the seam allowances converge at four different central points in the block.

If you press the rotating seam allowances in different directions, the points on your block will be sharp, but the central point will be needlessly bulky. You can reduce the bulk created by these seam allowances if you press them in the same direction around the central point. When you are developing a pressing plan that includes rotating seams, always begin at a central point rather than a corner of the block.

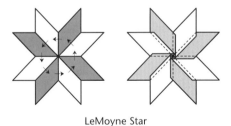

LeMoyne Star

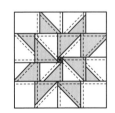

Diamond Star

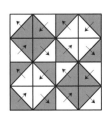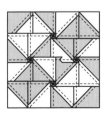

Shoo Fly

If you stitched through the central point when you assembled the block, you can remove the few stitches that prevent the seam allowances from folding back. Then press the seam allowances in a rosette, as shown below.

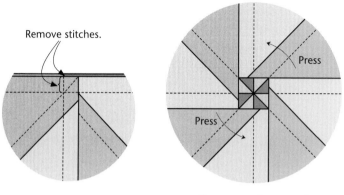

Press seam allowances in
a circle around center point,
then press open in a rosette.

Look at the blocks shown below. If you are making a Peace and Plenty block, you can butt all the diagonal seam allowances and at the same time press them in a circle around the central point to create a flat, accurate block. With more complicated block designs, such as Port and Starboard, you can press one or more intersecting seam allowances (usually the central seam) straight, and press the others in a circle. This way, you get the most possible benefit and manage to maintain your sanity. With rotating patterns, you can start to suffer from the Every Center Is Gonna Rotate strain of the IGBNMW syndrome—it just can't be done every time with every quilt.

Pressing Bias Edges

For best results, press on the straight of grain. If the pieces or strips have bias edges (such as with bias strip sets), rotate the tip of the iron 45° and press on the straight of grain. This helps avoid stretching the fabric edge or seam.

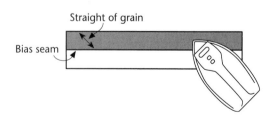

Straight of grain

Bias seam

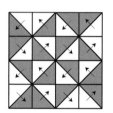

Peace and Plenty

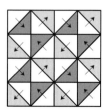
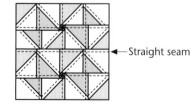

Straight seam

Port and Starboard

Diamonds and Hexagons

To make designs such as Tumbling Blocks, you stitch diamond-shaped pieces together to make hexagons, then stitch the hexagons together to make a tumbling block. Press the seam allowances in a circle around the central point. When you stitch the Tumbling Blocks together to make the quilt top, press the seam allowances in a circle around a new central point.

You can also apply this type of pressing plan to Grandmother's Flower Garden and other quilt patterns based on hexagons.

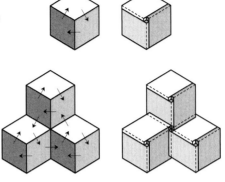

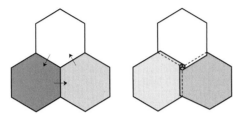

Grandmother's Flower Garden

Tumbling Blocks

Curves

Curved seams are another, more complex aspect of piecing and pressing. The Drunkard's Path block is a perfect example of how convex and concave curves fit together. When you lay the pieces side by side, the curves fit together precisely. However, to stitch these pieces together, you need to fit the concave piece into the convex piece. The seam allowance usually lies flatter if you press toward the concave curve. If you press the seam allowance toward the convex curve, you have to snip away some of the bulk to prevent creases and tucks in the seam line.

Generally, press all the curved seam allowances in the same direction. When you are making blocks with curved seam allowances as well as pieced sections, such as Baby Bunting and Rising Sun, press the curved seam allowances away from the section with the most piecing. If you press the seam allowances toward this section, you create needless bulk and make the surface of your block look bumpy.

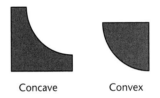

Concave   Convex

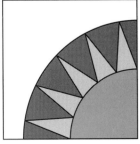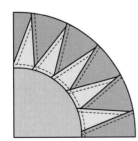

Baby Bunting

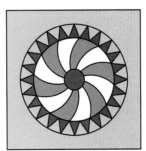

Rising Sun

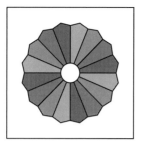
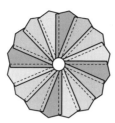

Many quilters appliqué the curved pieces in blocks such as Dresden Plate and Grandmother's Fan to the background fabric. Since this results in pressing seam allowances back against themselves, a better approach might be to appliqué the background fabric to the pieced section. Press the seam allowances away from the pieced section, toward the concave curve.

Dresden Plate

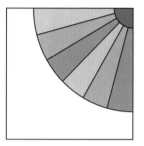
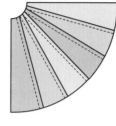

Segmented Blocks

Mariner's Compass; St. Louis Star; Morning Star, Evening Star; and Flower Pot are good examples of blocks that are assembled in segments. When you are making this type of block, think about the direction of the seam allowances in each segment and how they will interact with the seam allowances in adjoining segments. For example, there are eight segments in the Mariner's Compass block. All the seam allowances are pressed in the same direction around a central point.

Grandmother's Fan

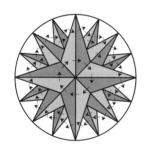

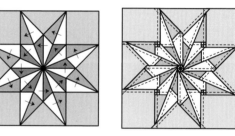

Mariner's Compass

St. Louis Star

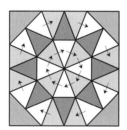
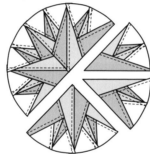

Morning Star, Evening Star

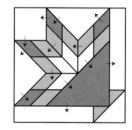
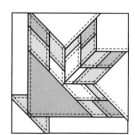

Flower Pot

Many complicated-looking blocks are simple to piece when you use a pressing plan. For example, I pieced two Mariner's Compass blocks for this book. I made one block using a foundation-piecing method and one block following a pressing plan. The block I assembled using foundation piecing had bulky seam allowances, and I had to struggle to make sharp points. The block I assembled following a pressing plan was incredibly (not just a little, but incredibly) easy to put together.

GALLERY

Delectable Mountains by Myrna Giesbrecht, 1995,
Kamloops, British Columbia, Canada, 34" x 34".
Every once in a while you make a quilt that's
just a little more special than the rest.
I really love the interaction of this marbled
background fabric with the clear, deep colors of
the main fabrics. Quilted by Carol Seely.

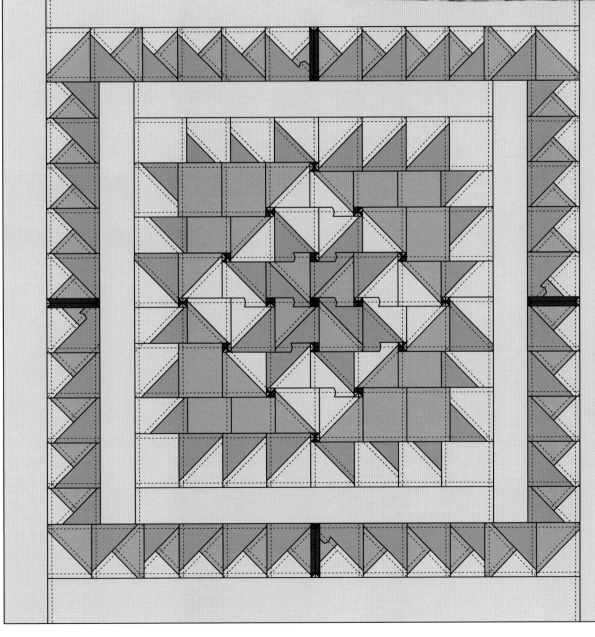

Four Patch by Myrna Giesbrecht, 1995, Kamloops, British Columbia, Canada, 23" x 29". Basic doesn't have to mean boring. Textured fabrics, a hint of gold metallic, and wavy quilting lines give life to this simple design. Quilted by Carol Seely.

Stars by Myrna Giesbrecht, 1995, Kamloops, British Columbia, Canada, 43" x 43".
Pieced in 1992 at Mary Ellen Hopkins's seminar "A Trip to the Amusement Park."
Large prints are great for designs like this. After being cut up, they really "twinkle."
Quilted by Carol Seely.

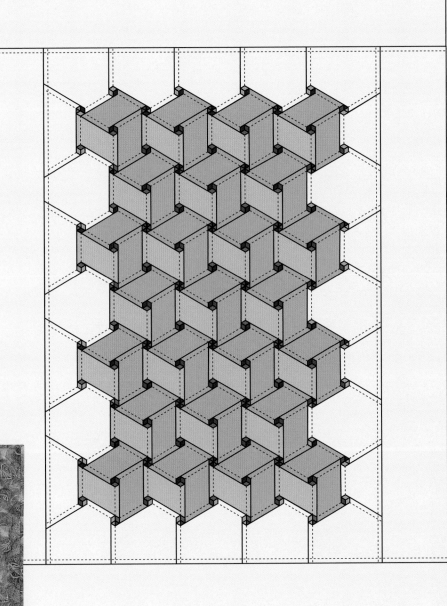

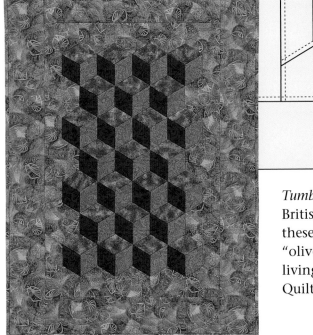

Tumbling Blocks by Myrna Giesbrecht, 1995, Kamloops, British Columbia, Canada, 28" x 37". I fell in love with these fabrics and couldn't resist. They mark the start of my "olive and lime green" phase. In fact, I've designed my living room around a plum carpet and lime green couch! Quilted by Carol Seely.

Foundation-Pieced Blocks

Though the variety and scope of foundation-pieced blocks is great, there are two drawbacks. First, if you've pieced to paper, you need to remove it when you're done. Using a smaller stitch length makes removing the paper easier and puts less stress on the seam. Creasing the paper over the stitches before you remove it also helps. Second, you have little or no control over the relationship of seam allowances between blocks. Therefore, while it might be quick and easy to piece each block, it might be more work to assemble the quilt top.

If you are making a foundation-pieced block, such as Log Cabin, press the seam allowances toward the edges of the block.

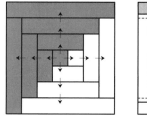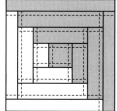

Log Cabin

SETTINGS

There are two basic quilt block settings: straight and diagonal. A diagonal setting is simply a straight setting turned 45°—so the blocks are on point. The seam allowances intersect at the same angle in either setting.

Developing a pressing plan makes it easier to join your blocks in rows and to add sashings and borders. When you are developing your pressing plan, be sure to indicate the top, bottom, and sides of every block. This ensures that the blocks are placed correctly when you join the rows.

The following sections explain the basic traffic patterns for setting your pieced blocks side by side, with plain blocks, with other pieced blocks, and with sashing.

Fold-Overs and Tucks

No matter how carefully you work, there will be times when you have a fold-over. That's when a seam ends up flipped and stitched, and it's not supposed to be. If your first inclination is to just leave it—don't! Fold-overs create bumps in the quilt top that interfere with quilting.

Remove the stitches in the seam allowance, flip it over, and re-stitch it as shown.

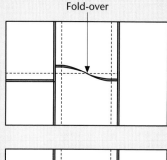

Fold-over

Small tucks or puckers along the seam line can sometimes be eased out by pushing them with a thumbnail, much like gathering on a blouse. It's worth a try!

Use thumbnail to ease slight puckering.

Block to Block

Even if you're using the same block throughout the quilt top, more than one traffic pattern might be needed. You will often need to develop *mirror pressing plans*; that is, you will have to press seam allowances in blocks that will be placed side by side in opposite directions. This ensures that the seams will butt when the rows are stitched together.

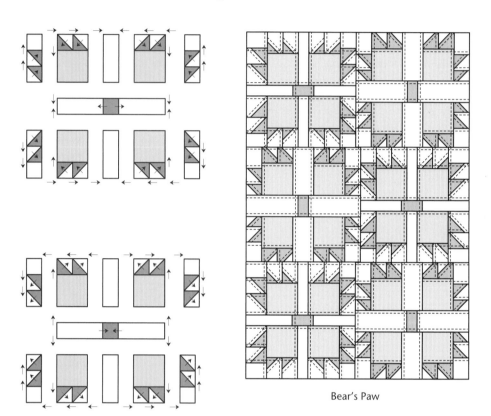

Bear's Paw

This is not the only potential traffic pattern. When joining a plain block with a pieced block, the ideal solution is to press the seam allowances toward the plain block. This reduces the bulk of pressing the seam allowances back on themselves.

 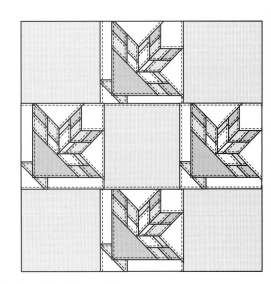

Press toward block containing the least number of seam allowances.

When joining two different pieced blocks, press the seam allowances toward the block that contains the larger pieces and fewer seam allowances. If there isn't much difference between the number of seam allowances, alternate the direction in which you press the seam allowances.

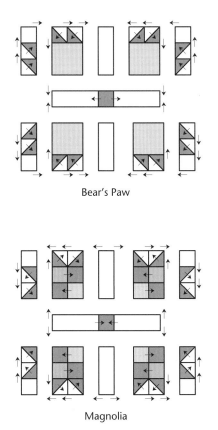

Bear's Paw

Magnolia

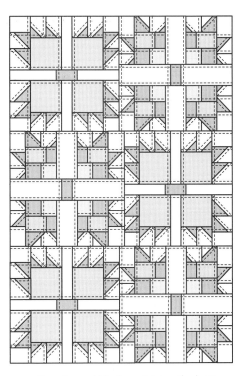

Press toward block containing the least number of seam allowances.

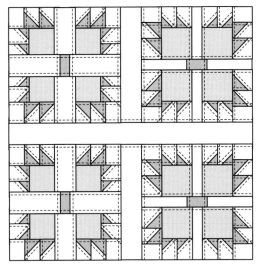

Press seam allowances toward sashing strips.

Sashing and Setting Squares

In a simple setting, plain strips of fabric separate the blocks and rows. Because there are no seam allowances within the sashing strips, it's a simple matter to press the seam allowances toward the sashing strips.

If you are using setting squares and sashing strips, press the seam allowances away from the setting squares toward the sashing strips. Press the seam allowances between the sashing strips and the blocks toward the sashing. When you join the rows of blocks and sashing strips, the seam allowances will butt.

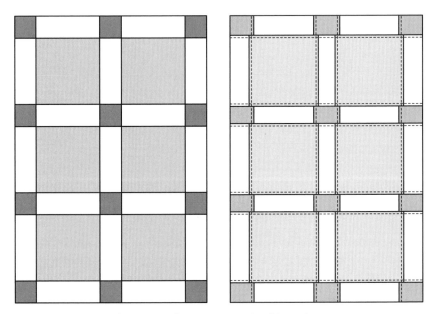

Press seam allowances toward sashing strips.

If you are using pieced sashing and setting squares, butt the sashing strip and setting square seam allowances as well as the block seam allowances wherever possible. For example, look at the illustration of triple sashing strips and Nine Patch setting squares below. In this example, the seam allowances are pressed toward the darker fabric.

Joining the Blocks

To help you remember which way is up, place a pin on the top of each block. Remove the pins once you've joined the blocks to avoid harming yourself.

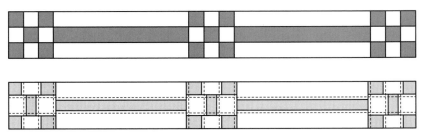

Butt seam allowances within setting squares and pieced sashing.

BORDERS

Few quilt tops are completed without border strips. Quilt borders range from very plain to immensely complicated.

Plain Borders

The easiest border design consists of strips of fabric. After you attach each border strip, set and press the seam allowances toward the strip. Then trim the excess fabric, if necessary, and attach the next border strip.

If you need to piece strips to achieve the desired length, use a mitered seam and press the seam allowances open (see page 35). This method makes it harder to see the seam.

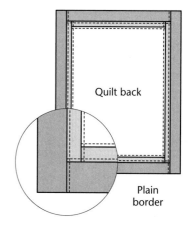

Plain border

Mitered Borders

If you are attaching mitered borders, press the top and bottom seam allowances opposite the side seam allowances. As you join the border strips to the center section, press the seam allowances toward the border strips. When you stitch the border strips together with mitered seams, the seam allowances butt.

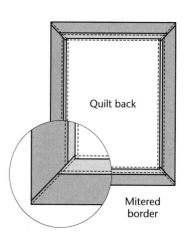

Mitered border

Accent Borders

Sometimes the construction technique dictates the direction of the seam allowances. Narrow $1/4$"-wide accent borders are a good example. When you are attaching narrow border strips, the edge of the presser foot must follow along the stitching line. If you have pressed the seam allowances toward the accent border strip, you may not be able to follow this line. Instead, press the seam allowances toward the center of the quilt top then re-press the seam allowances toward the second border.

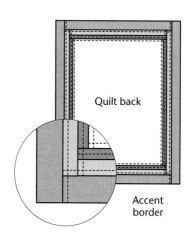

Accent border

Pieced Borders

When you are developing a pressing plan that includes pieced borders, focus first on the seam allowances in the pieced border. (Depending on the complexity of your design, you might want to develop a pressing plan just for the border.) Try to reduce bulk and butt seam allowances wherever possible so the border lies flat and smooth when you attach it to the quilt top. Next, look at the relationship between the seam allowances in the center section and the border. Again, try to reduce bulk and butt seam allowances.

Butt angled, vertical, and horizontal seam allowances within the pieced border to those within the central design wherever possible.

The width of the inner plain border equals one block in the pieced border.

When you want to add a pieced border, remember that there is more than one way to solve most problems. The solution to a difficult traffic pattern might be to press some seam allowances open or to add a plain border. An inner, plain border made from the center-section background fabric provides a seam-free edge for the pieced border. If possible, calculate the width of the inner border so you only need to add one or two blocks to the pieced border.

Round Robin Borders

Round Robin quilts are based on a central design and border after border, each of which may be designed and constructed by a different quilter. Since each quilter usually has no idea what the other quilters will do, you can't develop an integrated pressing plan until after the fact. However, this is not unusual. Border designs tend to stand alone. When you are trying to blend seam allowances from multiple borders and/or a central design, follow the pressing suggestions above.

Turning the Corner

Many quilts are "corner challenged" in terms of design, piecing, and pressing. The seam allowances in the corner blocks often won't butt against the seam allowances in both adjoining strips. If this is the case, press the seam allowances open or butt one end against a border strip and clip and flip the other end to butt the other border strip.

FINISHING UP

Once you've assembled your quilt top, recheck the seam allowances to make sure they are neat and correctly positioned. Working on the back side of the quilt top, reposition and re-press any errors and remove excess threads and fabric snippets. Gently press the seam allowances; use a shot of steam to set them. Turn the quilt top over and give it a final press. Be careful not to disturb the seam allowances and to work with the straight grain of the fabrics. For a crisper look, treat the quilt top with spray starch before pressing.

Hang the completed quilt top over a railing or shower rod to keep it wrinkle-free. If you must fold it, try to fold as few times as possible. Hang the folded quilt top on a padded clothes hanger.

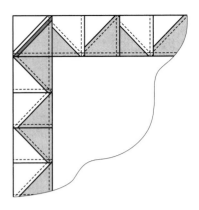

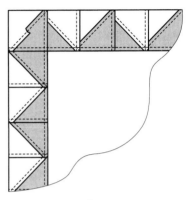

Press seam allowances open
or clip and flip to butt corner.

Backing

Seam allowances on a standard pieced backing are commonly pressed open to avoid layering seam allowances within the backing and the quilt top. I recommend developing a pressing plan for more complex pieced backs.

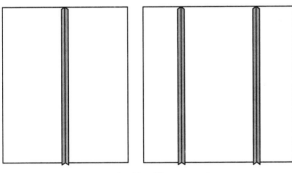

Standard backings

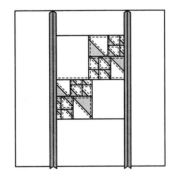

Pieced backing

Binding

Both straight-of-grain and bias binding strips are usually joined with bias seams. Press the seam allowances open to eliminate bulk and make it easier to stitch around corners.

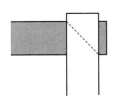

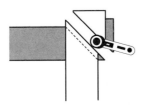

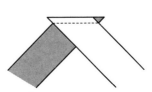

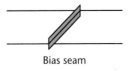

Bias seam

PRESSING PLAN EXERCISES AND SOLUTIONS

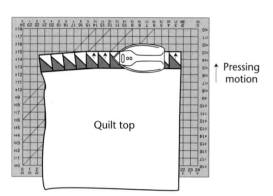

These exercises and solutions will help you learn to develop pressing plans based on the techniques and traffic patterns discussed in this book. Use them for any project. With practice, you'll be able to see and enjoy the benefits.

EXERCISES

Use these exercises to develop your own pressing plans. Remember that the goal of every pressing plan is to eliminate bulk and butt seam allowances wherever possible.

My pressing solutions for the same quilts are on pages 47–51. Do these exercises, then take a look at my pressing solutions.

Before you begin, refer to "Developing a Pressing Plan" on page 16. Exercises 1 and 2 are based on designs with squares and rectangles (see page 19). Exercise 3 adds triangles (see page 20). Exercises 4 and 5 focus on rotating patterns (see page 21). Exercise 6 is based on diamonds and hexagons (see page 23).

So grab a pencil and eraser and get started. Make arrows all over the place. I guarantee you'll learn a lot.

EXERCISE 1: FOUR PATCH

Make:

Press:

1. Determine the direction of the horizontal and vertical seam allowances within the Four Patch blocks. There are 2 traffic patterns for the block.

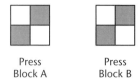

Press
Block A

Press
Block B

2. Using the letter *A* or *B* to indicate the traffic pattern, label all the squares to show the placement of the blocks. Also, determine the direction of the vertical seam allowances between the blocks in each row.

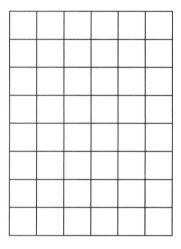

3. Determine the direction of the seam allowances joining the rows and the borders.

EXERCISE 2: STARS

This design uses the Connector Corner method described on page 13.

Make:

Press:

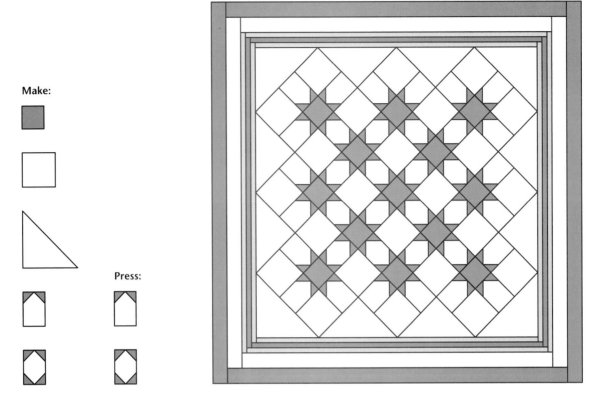

1. Determine the direction of the vertical seam allowances.

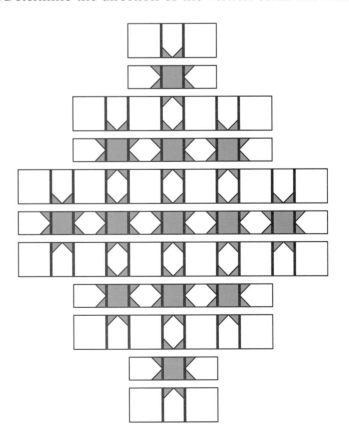

2. Determine the direction of the horizontal seam allowances.

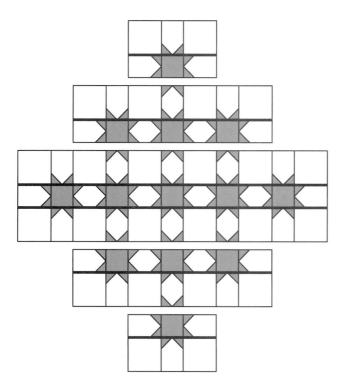

3. Determine the direction of the seam allowances joining the corner triangles, rows, and borders.

Exercise 3: Delectable Mountains

There are many variables to think about in this quilt design, including half- and quarter-square triangles, diagonal seam allowances, rotating intersections, and straight and pieced borders.

Make:

Press:

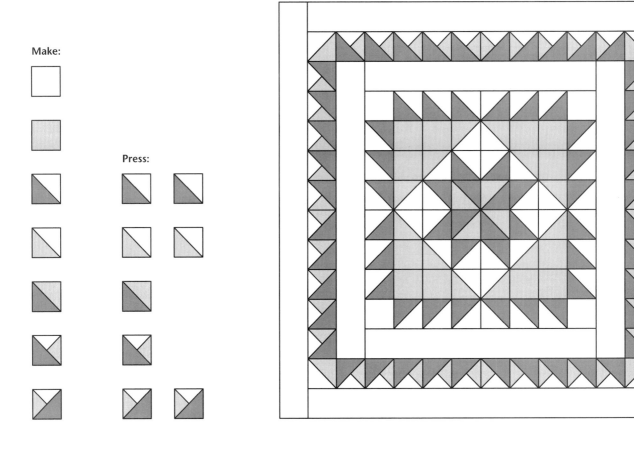

1. Determine which seam allowances should rotate.
2. Determine the direction of the diagonal seam allowances.

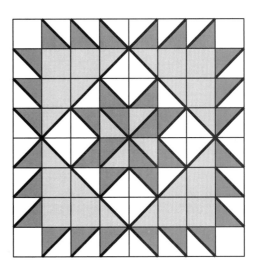

3. Determine the direction of the vertical seam allowances.

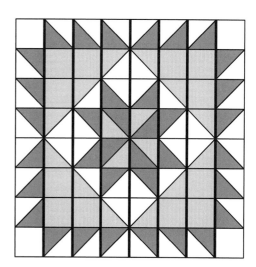

4. Determine the direction of the horizontal seam allowances.

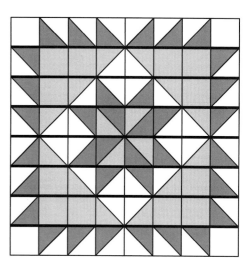

5. Determine the direction of the seam allowances for the pieced middle border.

6. Determine the direction of the seam allowances joining the inner, pieced, and outer borders.

Exercise 4: Spinning Stars

Two different pieced segments are repeated to make the Spinning Star block. Focus on rotating patterns in the blocks and on the sashing strips and setting squares.

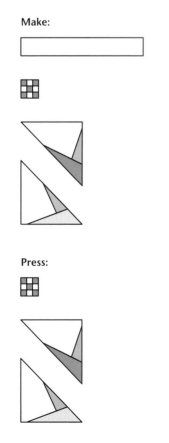

Make:

Press:

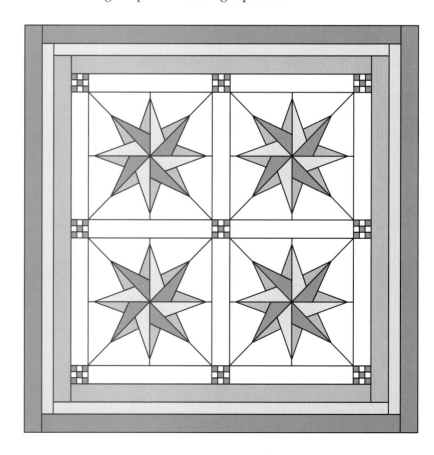

1. Determine the direction of the seam allowances within the 2 segments.

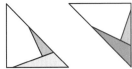

2. Determine the direction of the seam allowances within the pieced block.

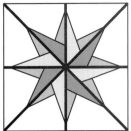

3. Determine the direction of the seam allowances in the Nine Patch blocks.

4. Determine the direction of the seam allowances for the sashing strips joining the blocks and setting squares.

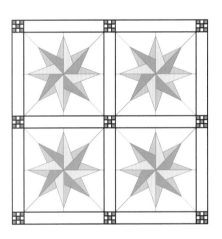

5. Determine the direction of the seam allowances for the inner, middle, and outer borders.

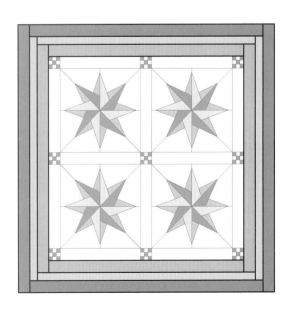

EXERCISE 5: MARINER'S COMPASS

Two different pieced segments are repeated to make the Mariner's Compass block. Focus on rotating patterns in the block and pieced border, which is made of half-star units, squares, rectangles, and triangles.

Make:

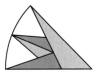

Press:

1. Determine the direction of the seam allowances within the 2 segments.

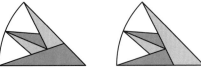

2. Determine the direction of the seam allowances within the pieced block.

3. Determine the direction of the seam allowances in the half-star units, then for the remainder of the pieced border.

4. Determine the direction of the seam allowances for the outer border.

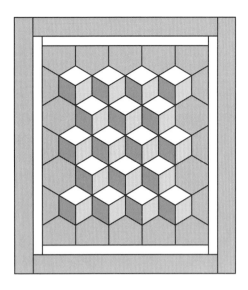

EXERCISE 6: TUMBLING BLOCKS

This design is based on diamonds and hexagons. Focus on rotating patterns.

Make:

Press:

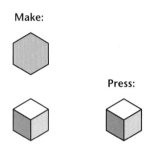

1. Determine the direction of the seam allowances within a pieced block.

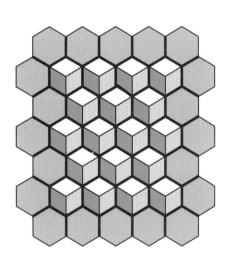

2. Determine the direction of the seam allowances joining the blocks to make the Tumbling Blocks design. *Note: I trim the edges to make the center a rectangle before adding the borders.*

3. Determine the direction of the seam allowances joining the inner and outer borders.

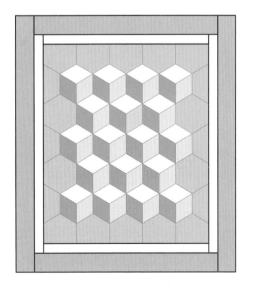

SOLUTIONS

I developed these pressing plans while making these quilts. If you came up with different pressing solutions while doing the exercises, don't assume that yours are wrong. (Remember that your pressing plans could mirror mine if you decided to press the first seam allowance in the opposite direction.) If you do find any major errors in your pressing-plan exercises, use my samples to correct them. As you gain experience, you'll develop your favorite way of doing things—your way, which naturally will be the easiest!

EXERCISE 1: FOUR PATCH

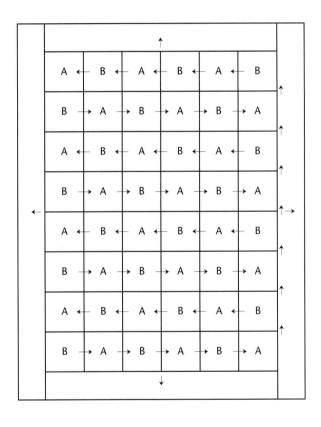

Block A
24

Block B
24

EXERCISE 2: STARS

Since I used the Connector Corner method on page 13 to make the pieced rectangle units, all my seam allowances are straight (rather than diagonal). This method, and my decision to press seam allowances toward the squares of feature fabric, simplifies quilt construction and highlights the Star blocks.

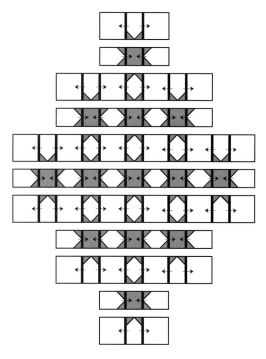

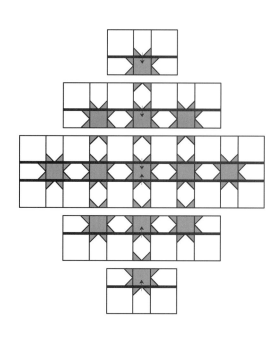

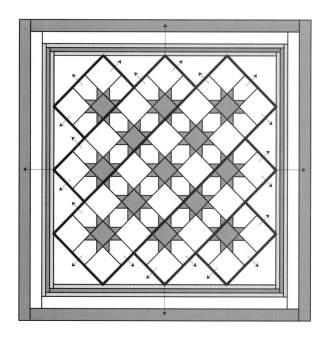

EXERCISE 3: DELECTABLE MOUNTAINS

I used half-square triangle units and squares to make the center of this quilt top, then added a plain inner border, a pieced middle border, and a plain outer border. I used half- and quarter-square triangle units to make the middle border.

There are 13 rotating intersections in and around the Pinwheel Star block. I pressed open or clipped and reversed some of the seam allowances

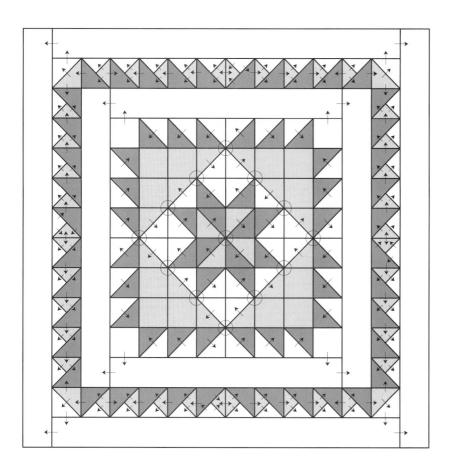

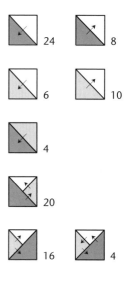

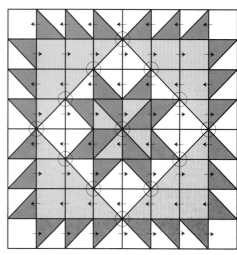

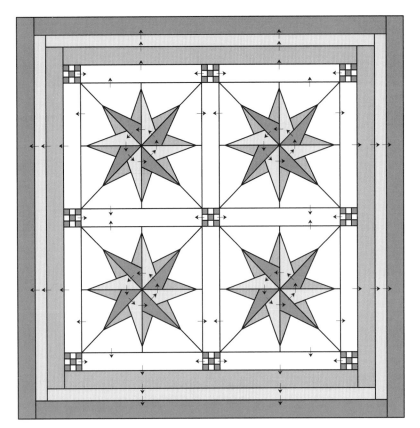

EXERCISE 4: SPINNING STARS

The sharp points of these Spinning Star blocks are much easier to make when you use a pressing plan. When you work with long bias pieces like these, it's a good idea to square each quarter-section before stitching them together (see page 51).

9

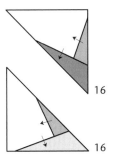

16

16

EXERCISE 5: MARINER'S COMPASS

Even complicated blocks, such as the Mariner's Compass, are easy to make if you piece, press, and square accurately. I had never made this block until I stitched this sample. It was so easy that I wondered why I'd put off making one for so long.

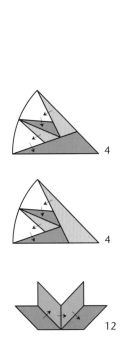

4

4

12

EXERCISE 6: TUMBLING BLOCKS

As I stitched the diamonds together to make each Tumbling Block, I pressed the seam allowances in a circle around a central point. All the seam allowances butt. I pressed seam allowances in a circle around other central points when I joined the blocks.

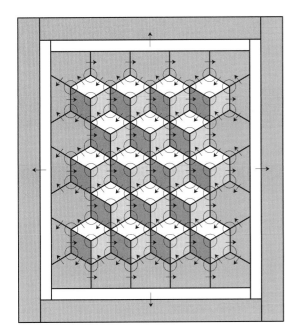

18

Poufy Centers

No matter how accurately you cut, stitch, and press, bias pieces can become distorted. To avoid "poufy" centers in blocks with long bias pieces, such as Spinning Stars and Mariner's Compass, use a rotary cutter and Bias Square® ruler to square each quarter-section of the block before stitching them together.

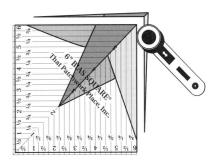

Square quarter-sections
before stitching block together.

MEET THE AUTHOR

Press for Success is my first book with That Patchwork Place. I've also written three other books: *Triangle Delight, Setting Up Your Sewing Space: From Small Areas to Complete Workshops*, and *Strip Quilts in a Hurry*.

When I'm not quilting and writing, I like to walk, read, go camping, do lunch, fabric shop, redecorate, and talk on the phone. My husband and I have three wonderful children: a girl and two boys, ages nine, six, and two. We're very proud of them. We live, play—and quilt—in Kamloops, British Columbia, Canada.

PRESSING RESOURCE

Spaceboard™
Voster Marketing
190 Mount Pleasant Road
Newton, CT 06470
1-800-231-1959 or (203) 270-7190

BIBLIOGRAPHY

Beyer, Jinny. *The Quilter's Album of Blocks & Borders.* McLean, Va.: EPM Publications, Inc., 1980 and 1986.

Dietrich, Mimi, and Roxi Eppler. *The Easy Art of Appliqué: Techniques for Hand, Machine, and Fusible Appliqué.* Bothell, Wash.: That Patchwork Place, 1994.

Hickey, Mary, Nancy J. Martin, Marsha McCloskey, and Sara Nephew. *Quick & Easy Quiltmaking: 26 Projects Featuring Speedy Cutting and Piecing Methods.* Bothell, Wash.: That Patchwork Place and Rodale Press, 1993.

Hopkins, Judy. *Around the Block with Judy Hopkins: 200 Rotary-Cut Blocks in 6 Sizes.* Bothell, Wash.: That Patchwork Place, 1994.

Hopkins, Mary Ellen. "A Trip to the Amusement Park," seminar. Las Vegas, Nev.: March 1992.

Magaret, Pat Maixner, and Donna Ingram Slusser. *Round Robin Quilts: Friendship Quilts of the '90s and Beyond.* Bothell, Wash.: That Patchwork Place, 1994.

Magaret, Pat Maixner, and Donna Ingram Slusser. *Watercolor Quilts.* Bothell, Wash.: That Patchwork Place, 1993.

Martin, Nancy J. *Fun with Fat Quarters.* Bothell, Wash.: That Patchwork Place, 1994.

Peters, Paulette. *Borders by Design.* Bothell, Wash.: That Patchwork Place, 1994.

Quilted for Christmas. Compiled by Ursula Reikes. Bothell, Wash.: That Patchwork Place, 1994.

Schneider, Sally. *Painless Borders.* Bothell, Wash.: That Patchwork Place, 1992.

Thomas, Donna Lynn. *A Perfect Match.* Bothell, Wash.: That Patchwork Place, 1993.

Thomas, Donna Lynn. *Shortcuts to the Top.* Bothell, Wash.: That Patchwork Place, 1994.

Townswick, Jane. *Quiltmaking Tips and Techniques: Over 1,000 Creative Ideas to Make Your Quiltmaking Quicker, Easier and a Lot More Fun.* Edited by Suzanne Nelson. Emmaus, Pa.: Rodale Press, 1994.